D0046843

THE BANTAM LIBRARY
of Culinary Arts ™

Aromatic HERBS

JILL NORMAN

BANTAM BOOKS
TORONTO · NEW YORK · LONDON · SYDNEY · AUCKLAND

AROMATIC HERBS

A BANTAM BOOK/PUBLISHED BY ARRANGEMENT WITH
DORLING KINDERSLEY LIMITED

PRINTING HISTORY
DORLING KINDERSLEY EDITION
PUBLISHED IN GREAT BRITAIN IN 1989

BANTAM EDITION/MAY 1990

EDITOR GWEN EDMONDS
DESIGNER MATTHEWSON BULL
PHOTOGRAPHER DAVE KING

ART DIRECTOR STUART JACKMAN

LIBRARY OF CONGRESS CATALOGING-IN-PUBLICATION DATA

NORMAN, JILL.
AROMATIC HERBS:
HOW TO USE THEM IN COOKING AND SEASONING FOODS /
JILL NORMAN. — BANTAM ED.
P. CM. — (THE BANTAM LIBRARY OF CULINARY ARTS)
"DORLING KINDERSLEY EDITION PUBLISHED IN GREAT BRITAIN 1989" — T.P. VERSO
INCLUDES INDEX.
ISBN 0—553—05741—3
1. COOKERY (HERBS). I. TITLE. II. SERIES.
TX819.H4N67 1990
641.6′57–DC20
89—6879   CIP

PRINTED AND BOUND IN HONG KONG
0 9 8 7 6 5 4 3

CONTENTS

INTRODUCTION

"Speak not – whisper not;
Here bloweth thyme and bergamot;
Softly on the evening hour,
Secret herbs their spices shower,
Dark-spiked rosemary and myrrh,
Lean-stalked, purple lavender;"

The Sunken Garden, *Walter de la Mare*

*E*VERYONE CAN GROW HERBS, *whether in the garden, window boxes or containers. Most herbs prefer well-drained soil and a sunny position. Sunlight develops their volatile oils, which produce the plant's characteristic scent and flavor. The sweet smell of herbs in summer is one of the most agreeable things about growing them, and their flavors are readily transferred to a variety of dishes. Aromatic herbs are mostly used in cooked dishes, and many may be used fresh or dried, though not necessarily interchangeably. You could not make a mint julep with dried mint, but dried mint is more successful than fresh in many dishes such as the Turkish kofte on page 35.*

These days a wide range of fresh herbs is available year round from many supermarkets if you don't grow your own. Some herbs keep well for a few days in a pot of water – coriander and parsley do particularly well; most keep up to a week in a loose plastic bag in the refrigerator, and many, coriander, mint and horseradish among them, will freeze well if chopped and packed in small plastic pots, but frozen herbs should only be added to a dish for the last few minutes of its cooking time.

Parsley, basil and coriander do not dry well, and dried tarragon has a less potent flavor than fresh. Mint, marjoram, oregano and rosemary do dry well and have a more concentrated flavor. So if you substitute dried for fresh herbs, do so sparingly. Dried herbs do not keep their aroma indefinitely – about a year is the maximum time, so only buy in small amounts.

To dry your own, gather the herbs on a dry day before the flowering time because the flavor is strongest then. Tie them in bundles and hang in a dark airy place or spread them on paper in a cupboard. It is not a good idea to dry them in a low oven unless forced to do so because of bad weather. Drying will take 10 to 20 days depending on the plant and the conditions. Strip the leaves from the stalks and store in air-tight jars. It is useful to keep small quant-

Commercial drying of herbs, c. 1923

ities of dried herb mixtures too. Mrs Grieve recommends "equal proportions of knotted marjoram and winter savory with half quantities of basil, thyme and tarragon, all rubbed to a powder" in Culinary Herbs and Condiments, 1934. Equal amounts of powdered rosemary, thyme, winter savory, bay leaves and grated lemon rind make a good seasoning for stuffing and stews, and for a fashionable Cajun flavor from Louisiana combine equal quantities of crushed thyme, oregano and basil with ground black and red chili pepper and salt.

BASIL

*O*CIMUM BASILICUM *is a tropical member of the mint family, with a spicy flavor and scent. Best used fresh but will keep in a jar with olive oil and a little salt. Asian varieties, used sparingly in India but abundantly in Thai cooking, are more pungent than those from cooler climates.*

Ocimum basilicum

Fresh basil goes well with tomatoes, raw or cooked. Eggplant and pepper dishes benefit from basil, as does a good firm fish such as mullet or sea bass. Combined with garlic it gives a peppery flavor to plain chicken dishes and, as pesto, makes the ultimate pasta sauce. Basil vinegar brightens many a winter salad.

BAY

*T*HE TOUGH LEAVES *of the laurel tree* (Laurus nobilis), *and in India the mellower ones of the cassia tree, are used fresh or dried to impart a spicy aroma to many different dishes. In medieval Europe bay was a popular strewing herb, for its scent and antiseptic properties. In Moghul pilafs it is one of the four essential spices.*

Bay leaves are basic to much Mediterranean and French cooking, in marinades and pickles, court bouillon, bouquet garni, stews and the milk used for cream sauces.

The fresh leaves can often be a little bitter, but the bitterness (unlike the scent) fades quickly. Leaves should be dried in the dark to retain their color.

Laurus nobilis

BERGAMOT

*M*ONARDA DIDYMA, *also called bee balm, is a North American member of the mint family. As "Oswego tea" (from its Indian origin) it became popular in the New World after the Boston Tea Party of 1773 and, not much later, even in England. Fresh, it adds spice to fruit cups.*

Bergamot must be used sparingly but is good in salads (both leaves and bright flowers) or stuffings and to flavor jams, jellies and the milk used for puddings.

The whole plant gives off a pleasant lemony fragrance and for this reason has long been a favorite in garden borders. Its culinary use has on the whole been sadly neglected.

Monarda didyma

CORIANDER

*A*LTHOUGH CORIANDER (CORIANDRUM SATIVUM) *has been well-known in China and India for thousands of years, it was Arab cooking that spread the use of both the herb and its small seed through the Middle East, North Africa, Spain and Portugal and from there to the New World.*

Known as "Chinese parsley" but called "the fragrant plant" in China itself, where it is much used chopped up fine in sauces. In India the seed is essential; from the Middle East westward herb and seed are equal partners. The herb is normally used fresh. It does not dry, but freezes well or can be kept, like basil, preserved with salt in oil. It does not take well to long cooking, and it is therefore best added at a late stage. India and South America use the excellent combination of coriander and green chilies in chutneys and sauces. Soups, salads and stuffings benefit greatly from it. Thai cuisine uses the roots to flavor stews.

Coriandrum
sativum

GARLIC

A LLIUM SATIVUM *is a staple of everyday cooking for all but the Anglo-Saxons. A tonic and a seasoning, with great warming qualities, it balances sharper flavors such as ginger or chili. Make sure you buy hard cloves that are free of spots.*

Raw garlic has a strong taste; cooked it is mild and leaves no trace on the breath. When frying, remove garlic before it browns.

Allium sativum

The basis of strong sauces such as aïoli and rouille, and the more subtle flavoring in many meat, game and fish recipes, garlic blends well with many vegetables and with most herbs and spices. Slow-cooked heads make a mellow accompaniment to roasts.

HORSERADISH

*A*RMORACIA RUSTICANA *is easily recognizable by its large crinkly leaves which grow, palmlike, straight up from the root, or in summer by its white flowers on their long spike. It is not easy to dig up, as it develops a rather complex root system – and it is the roots that are used.*

Scrubbed (or, if you want pure white horseradish, peeled) and grated – a process more eye watering than onion peeling – it may be used instantly, but its active life can be prolonged by making a sauce with yogurt or cream and some sugar and vinegar, or blending to a staple condiment with dry mustard, water, salt and pepper.

Armoracia rusticana

LOVAGE

L EVISTICUM OFFICINALE *is a rather neglected herb that was popular in classical Greece and Rome. Its wild form, growing along Atlantic coasts, was used as a vegetable in Scotland and America. The stems can be candied; the seeds give a taste of celery to whole wheat bread.*

A few fresh leaves will liven up a green salad and, shredded, go well with tomato and egg dishes. Try lovage butter with potatoes.

Lovage is a good addition to vegetable dishes. Its yeasty flavor gives an almost meaty taste, notably to beans but also to stuffings or sauces. It makes excellent soup by itself or can be used to flavor other soups.

Levisticum officinale

PARSLEY

$\mathcal{P}$ETROSELINUM CRISPUM *has become the standard decorative herb of the Anglo-Saxon world, while European cooking adds parsley almost as easily as salt, often as a last-minute "persillade" (with shallots) or "picada" (with nuts and garlic).*

Parsley is always used fresh. The stalks are an essential ingredient of bouquet garni, as the finely chopped leaves are of many sauces (often together with lemon or lemon balm) and a number of butters, including maître d'hôtel and garlic butter.

Indonesian cooking uses parsley (introduced by the Dutch), and in Turkey parsley omelettes herald the coming of spring. Parsley is decorative in aspic or deep-fried.

Petroselinum crispum

Petroselinum sativum

MARJORAM & OREGANO

*M*ARJORAM (ORIGANUM MAJORANA) *has been cultivated for its medicinal and culinary properties for many centuries in the Middle East. Introduced into Europe in medieval times its fragrance was valued for toilet waters. Today its use is confined to the kitchen, where often it is interchangeable with thyme. Sweet marjoram is not as hardy as the coarser pot marjoram.*

Origanum Majorana
Sweet marjoram

Origanum Onites
Pot
marjoram

Origanum vulgare
Oregano

Oregano (*O. vulgare*) is the common name for wild marjoram that grows from the Himalayas to the British Isles, and for unrelated plants with the same properties that grow in Mexico. In warm climates the herb is much more pungent and peppery than in cool wet ones. Both marjoram and oregano can be used when dried. In fact, the latter is not normally exported in any other form since it retains a remarkably concentrated flavor. The delicate flavor of sweet marjoram is easily lost in cooking: add it only toward the end. The fresh herb, chopped, with some lemon juice, makes a good dressing. Oregano provides the pungent flavoring of pizza. It goes particularly well with onion, eggplant, tomato, beans and meat.

O.v. aureum
Golden marjoram

O.v. Pink-flowered
marjoram

MINT

*M*INT (MENTHA SPECIES) *has been used as a flavoring herb since antiquity. From its native Mediterranean habitat it spread throughout Europe with the Roman legions. Many mints are cultivated or grow wild; the best for flavor is spearmint. Apple and Bowles' mints with their woolly-looking leaves are also popular in the kitchen. Peppermint makes a flavoring oil for sweets.*

Mentha spicata
Spearmint

Mentha spicata variegata
Variegated apple mint

Mint does not blend easily with other herbs, but its potent and refreshing flavor suits a wide range of other ingredients: the new potatoes and marrow-fat peas of England; dishes of mutton and lamb; the yogurt and cucumber salad of Turkey and the Balkans; sweet teas of India and Morocco or the equally sweet whisky-based mint julep of Kentucky. Mint is the main herb in Moghul cooking; it is widely used in India and the Middle East. It dries well, retaining its great strength.

M. × villosa
Bowles' mint

ROSEMARY

A NOTHER HERB *of Mediterranean origin,* Rosmarinus officinalis *grows well in other parts of Europe and in North America. It is an aromatic plant that thrives in any warm dry place, even with the poorest soil. Its leathery and spiky leaves have a strong flavor with a hint of pine needles but also of the camphor which is part of its essential oil. Rosemary, which has very pretty pale blue flowers during a long season, is an evergreen bush, so the herb is always available fresh.*

Rosmarinus officinalis

Rosemary is normally used whole, in sprigs, for the hard leaves are not very pleasant, and their taste, when chewed, is a little overpowering. It blends well with garlic and wine in marinades or cooking liquids for rabbit and other small game. Its traditional use is in roasting or grilling, mostly lamb or kid, but also fish and shellfish, especially on skewers over a barbecue.

SAGE

*T*HE MANY VARIETIES OF **Salvia officinalis**
*include both decorative and culinary plants.
Among the latter, the blue-
flowered and narrow-leaved variety and the usually nonflowering
broad-leaved ones are those commonly used. Names such as
pineapple, lavender or wormwood
sage hint at the differences
in flavor.*

Sage shares with rosemary the
reputation of being somewhat
crude (camphor is the culprit
again) but its usefulness goes
beyond sage and onion stuffing
to interesting dishes of eel, ham,
liver, sausages and veal, as well
as flavoring for beans or peas
and kebabs.

Salvia officinalis

SAVORY

*T*HE ROMANS *brought savory* (Satureja montana) *from the Mediterranean to the rest of Europe, and later, migrants took it to the New World. Summer and winter savory are but two of a number of species that were commonly used until the arrival of the stronger spices from the East. The spiky leaves are best before the flowering.*

The rather aggressive, peppery flavor of savory (which the dried herb retains) is traditionally used in sausages, stuffings, and with both fresh and dried beans. It goes well with cucumber, and blended with other herbs makes a good seasoning for fish.

Satureja montana

TARRAGON

Artemisia dracunculus's tangy and slightly bitter taste betrays its relation to wormwood. From its Middle Eastern origins it reached Europe only in the 16th century, century, via Moorish Spain. It is an herb with a variety of uses, from providing an appetizing scent on a barbecue fire to being frozen in ice cubes to flavor cold drinks.

French tarragon has a more subtle aroma and flavor than the Russian (*A. dracunculoides*). It can be used in roasting, or as tarragon butter with asparagus or artichokes.

Artemisia dracunculus

Tarragon vinegar, made by steeping the fresh herb in white wine vinegar for two months, is a fine kitchen staple for salad dressings, mustards and many sauces.

THYME

THE THYMUS SPECIES was named by the ancient Greeks, but probably even they were not the first to exploit its culinary properties. Many species, with varying flavors, grow wild in the hot and dry parts of western Asia, North Africa and southern Europe; others have been cultivated for cooler climates.

Thymus pulegioides
Broad leaf thyme

Thyme is an essential herb in most Western cooking. It is a standard component of bouquet garni and many a court bouillon, goes well with vegetables (from tomato to potato) and with fish or in stuffings. It withstands slow cooking in stews, where it blends easily with garlic, onion and brandy or red wine to give a deep aroma. It gives similar qualities to marinades for pork and large game, and even to a pickle for olives.

Thymus p. a. aureus
Golden creeping thyme

T. × citriodorus argenteus
Silver lemon thyme

Thyme dries quite well, but the more delicate components of its complex flavor seem to be subdued in the process. Several species are grown for decorative use (silver leaf, golden creeper) while others such as lemon thyme are valuable kitchen variants.

Thymus vulgaris
Common thyme

Thymus
Serpyllum
Wild thyme

T. × citriodorus
Lemon scented
thyme

Recipes

The recipes will serve 4,
but some (such as those for breads)
will serve more.

HERB BREAD
Use rosemary to flavor this
bread but sage, thyme or
marjoram work well too.

2/3 cup/175 ml milk
1 teaspoon salt
1/2 oz/15 g butter
1/2 packet dried yeast
1/4 oz/7 g ordinary dried yeast
3 cups/375 g white flour
2/3 cup/175 ml warm water
2 tablespoons finely chopped
fresh rosemary or 2 teaspoons dried

Heat the milk and stir in the salt
and butter until dissolved.
Sprinkle the yeast
over the warm water and let it
prove. Stir the water into the
flour, then the milk. Scatter the
rosemary over the mixture and
stir until well blended. The
dough should be quite soft and
batterlike, and it is easily mixed

with a wooden spoon. Cover
and let rise in a warm place
until at least doubled in bulk –
about 1 hour.
Stir and beat thoroughly for a
minute or so, then pour the
batter into a greased 8-in
loaf pan and bake at once in a
preheated oven, 180°C, 350°F
for about 1 hour. When it
is done the bottom should sound
hollow when tapped.
Cool on a rack
This bread will keep for a day or
so, but it is much better fresh.

FOCCACIA WITH SAGE

½ packet dried yeast
3 cups/375 g white flour
1 cup/250 ml warm water
1 teaspoon salt
2 tablespoons chopped fresh sage
leaves or 2 teaspoons dried
olive oil

Sprinkle the yeast over the
warm water and let it prove.
Mix the salt and sage into the
flour. Add 1 tablespoon oil and
the water and mix to a soft
dough. Knead on a floured
surface or in the bowl until you
have a springy, elastic dough.
Oil the bowl lightly and let the
dough rise for about 50 minutes
or until it has doubled in bulk.
On a floured surface, roll out
the dough to a circle 1-in
thick. Put the foccacia on a
greased baking sheet; make
some indentations in the surface
with your fingers and let
rise for 30 minutes. Brush with
olive oil, sprinkle and coarse
salt and bake in a preheated
oven, 190°C, 375°F for
about 40 minutes. Foccacia is
best eaten the day it is made.

Bouquet Garni

A few sprigs of thyme, a bay leaf and 2 or 3 fresh parsley stalks make up a standard bouquet garni, but a stalk of celery, a sprig of another herb such as lovage, marjoram or savory may be added. In Provence a strip of orange peel is common; for a fish dish a strip of lemon peel would be appropriate. The herbs are tied in a bundle so they can be removed at the end of the cooking time.

Tomato Sauce

1 small onion, chopped finely
2 tablespoons olive oil
2 cloves garlic, crushed
1 lb/500 g tomatoes, chopped
2 tablespoons tomato paste
1 sprig thyme
1 bay leaf
2 tablespoons chopped parsley
2/3 cup/150 ml white wine
3 tablespoons water
salt and pepper

Sauté the onion in oil until soft. Add the garlic and continue to cook, then 2 minutes later stir in the tomatoes, tomato paste, thyme, bay leaf and parsley. Season with salt and pepper, then pour in the wine and water. Stir thoroughly, cover and simmer for 20 minutes. Strain the sauce and serve.

Basil, Mint and Red Pepper Sauce

large handful of basil leaves
3–4 sprigs mint
1 sweet red pepper
3 tablespoons olive oil
2 tablespoons red wine vinegar
1 small clove garlic, chopped finely
salt and pepper

Strip the leaves from the mint sprigs and chop them finely with the basil leaves. Scorch the pepper over a gas flame or under a grill until it is blackened all over, then wrap in damp paper towels for a few minutes. The skin will then rub off easily. Remove the seeds and membranes and chop the flesh finely. Mix together the oil, vinegar, garlic and seasonings. Stir in the herbs and pepper. The sauce goes particularly well with cold fish, such as poached skate or turbot.

Horseradish, Apple and Beet Salad

2 oz/50 g horseradish, grated
3 tablespoons wine vinegar
1 tablespoon sugar
2 firm eating apples
3 tablespoons olive oil
1/2 lb/250 g cooked beets, cubed
fresh black pepper

Mix the horseradish, 2 tablespoons vinegar and the sugar together. Peel, quarter and slice the apples and mix with the horseradish. Add 2 tablespoons oil and blend thoroughly.

Toss the beets in the remaining oil and vinegar, season with black pepper. Pile it in the center of a dish and surround with the apple and horseradish.

Carrot Salad

Dress *grated carrot* with *olive oil* and *lemon juice*. Season with *salt* and *pepper* and finely chopped *lovage* or *coriander*. Toss and leave for half an hour for the flavors to blend.

27

PERSIAN CHICK PEA SOUP WITH MEAT BALLS

6 oz/175 g lean ground beef
1 onion, finely chopped
1/4 teaspoon cinnamon
salt and pepper
6 oz/175 g chick peas, soaked
overnight
4 oz/125 g lentils
2 leeks, sliced thinly
6 oz/175 g spinach, chopped
6 oz/175 g assorted fresh herbs –
lovage, mint, parsley, coriander,
dill, chopped
1 oz/25 g butter

Mix together thoroughly the meat, onion and cinnamon with salt and pepper to taste and make meatballs, the size of a walnut. Set them aside.
Put the chick peas in a large pan with 2½ pints water, bring to boil, then cover and simmer for 30 minutes. Add the meatballs and lentils and continue to cook for 30 minutes more. Then put in the leeks and spinach, simmer for another 20 minutes, add the herbs and cook for 10 minutes. Remove from the heat, stir in the butter and serve.

LOVAGE SOUP

1 oz/25 g butter
1 onion, chopped
2 tablespoons flour
2½ cups/600 ml chicken stock
3 tablespoons chopped lovage leaves
juice ½ lemon
salt and pepper
²/₃ cup/150 ml light cream

Melt the butter, cook the onion until soft, then add the flour and stir well. Pour in the stock, a little at a time, and stir until the soup has thickened somewhat. Add the lovage and lemon juice and simmer for 20 minutes. Season with salt and pepper, then purée in a blender or through a sieve. Stir in the cream, heat through gently and serve.

FISH SOUP WITH TARRAGON

1 large onion, sliced
white part of 2 leeks, sliced
1 large potato, diced
1 bay leaf
2 sprigs tarragon
salt, white pepper
¾ lb/375 g white fish fillets
²/₃ cup/150 ml light cream
1 tablespoon chopped fresh tarragon

Put the vegetables in a pan with the bay leaf, tarragon sprigs and 1 pint/600 ml water. Season with salt and pepper, bring to a boil and simmer, covered, for 10 minutes. Add the fish, cut in large pieces, and simmer until it will flake easily – about 8–10 minutes. Lift out the fish pieces and flake. Remove the bay leaf and tarragon sprigs. Stir the cream into soup and heat gently. Return the fish to the soup, heat through and serve sprinkled with chopped tarragon.

MUSSEL SALAD

2 lb/1kg mussels
2 onions
3 carrots
2 leeks
3 stalks celery
6 oz/175 g celeriac
2 cloves garlic
4 tablespoons olive oil
a large bunch of parsley
3 tomatoes, peeled and seeded
salt and pepper
lemon juice

Scrub the mussels and remove the beards, discarding any that are broken or open. Put them in a heavy pan over medium heat, cover with a lid and leave for 5 minutes or so until they open. Strain into a bowl, reserving the liquor.

Dice or chop all the vegetables finely. Chop the garlic and parsley. Soften the onion in the oil, then add the leeks, carrots, celery, celeriac and garlic. Cook for a few minutes, stirring to coat them with oil. Strain the mussel liquor twice through a cheesecloth and add about ¼ pint/150 ml to the vegetables. Cover and simmer gently until the vegetables are cooked. If necessary add a little more liquid. Remove the mussels from their shells, discarding any that haven't opened. Add the mussels and parsley to the vegetables and cook uncovered for 10 minutes so that the liquid reduces somewhat. Add the tomatoes; taste and season if necessary with salt and pepper. Turn into a serving dish, squeeze over a little lemon juice and let cool.

STUFFED SQUID

4 medium squid
1 oz/25 g dried mushrooms
1 small onion, chopped
2 tablespoons oil
3 oz/75 g rice, parboiled
1 teaspoon dried thyme
1 teaspoon dried oregano
grated rind of 2 lemons
salt and pepper
tomato sauce (p. 26)

Clean the squid: remove the pink filmy skin, the wings and the innards and head. Rinse the sacks well; cut the tentacles from the heads and chop finely with the wings.
Soak the mushrooms in hot water for 30 minutes. Heat the oil and fry the onion and chopped squid for 5 minutes over low heat. Add the drained rice, herbs and lemon rind. Drain the mushrooms, chop and add to the pan. Season well. Fill the squid pouches three quarters full and sew up the ends or fasten them with toothpicks. Cook the squid slowly in the tomato sauce for 30-40 minutes. Do not let them cook too quickly or the squid will be tough.

COD STEAKS WITH PARSLEY AND LEMON THYME

4 cod steaks
6 tablespoons dry bread crumbs
4 tablespoons chopped parsley
2 tablespoons chopped lemon thyme
salt and pepper
2 tablespoons olive oil

Combine the bread crumbs and herbs. Season the fish on both sides and brush with oil. Press some of the herb mixture firmly onto both sides of the steaks and drizzle more oil over them. Put the fish in a lightly oiled baking dish and cook for 8 minutes in a preheated oven, 200°C, 400°F. Finish the fish briefly under the grill to turn the coating crusty.
Serve with tomato sauce (p. 26).

STIR-FRIED THAI CHICKEN

3-4 chicken breasts, skinned and boned
1 tablespoon cornstarch
2 tablespoons brandy or sherry
2 tablespoons soy sauce
2 fresh red chilies, seeded and chopped
1 tablespoon rice vinegar
1 tablespoon sugar
1/2 teaspoon powdered lemongrass
2 tablespoons oil
1 onion, sliced thinly
a handful of basil leaves, chopped
a handful of mint leaves, chopped
1 lime, cut in wedges

Cut the chicken into cubes.
Whisk together the cornstarch
brandy, and 1 tablespoon soy
sauce and marinate the chicken
for 15 minutes. Combine the
remaining soy sauce with the
chilies, vinegar, sugar and
lemongrass and set aside.
Heat the oil in a wok and stir-fry
the onion and chicken for 2–3
minutes until the onions are soft
and the chicken starts to color.
Add the soy mixture and half
the basil and mint. Continue
stirring and turning for a minute
or two until the chicken is tender.
Transfer to a warm serving dish.
Scatter the remaining herbs
over the chicken and serve with
the wedges of lime.

Roast Pork with Sage

2 lb/1 kg pork loin, bones and skin
removed, and rolled
10 sage leaves
1 clove garlic, cut in slivers
large sprig thyme
1 bay leaf
salt
2 tablespoons olive oil

With the point of a sharp knife
pierce the meat on all sides and
insert the sage leaves and garlic
slivers. Strip the leaves from the
thyme and mix with the
crumbled bay leaf and salt. Rub
the meat with this mixture and
put it into a small roasting pan.
Pour over the oil and roast in a
preheated oven, 180°C, 350°F,
for 1 hour, basting
occasionally. Let the meat
rest for 10 minutes in a warm
place before carving.
The pork is also good cold with
a potato salad.

Rabbit with Rosemary

4 pieces rabbit
$2/3$ cup/150 ml olive oil
1 clove garlic, crushed
2-3 sprigs rosemary
juice $1/2$ lemon
$2/3$ cup/150 ml white wine
2 tomatoes, peeled, seeded and
chopped
salt and pepper
2 oz/50 g small black olives

Marinate the rabbit in the oil,
garlic, rosemary and lemon juice
for 6 to 8 hours, turning
occasionally. Transfer the rabbit
and the marinade to a heavy pan
and cook over a low heat for 20
minutes. Add the wine, bring to
the boil and reduce slightly,
then add the tomatoes. Season
with salt and pepper and simmer
for a further 25 minutes. Put in
the olives and cook for another 5
minutes. Remove the rosemary
sprigs and serve.

BŒUF EN DAUBE

2 lb/1 kg chuck beef
2 onions, quartered
2 carrots, sliced
2 bouquets garnis
1¼ cups/300 ml red wine
oil
4 oz/125 g salt pork
4 cloves garlic, crushed
strip of orange peel
pinch cayenne
salt and pepper

Cut the beef into 8–10 pieces and put in a bowl with the onion, carrot, a bouquet garni, salt, wine and 1 tablespoon oil. Marinate for 4–5 hours or longer, turning the meat occasionally.

Remove the rind from the salt pork and cut it into thin strips. Cut the salt pork in small cubes. Put another tablespoon of oil into an earthenware casserole, put in the salt pork and rinds, the drained meat and vegetables. Place the garlic cloves among the contents, put a new bouquet garni and a strip of orange peel in the middle of the casserole and season with pepper and a little cayenne. Pour over the marinade liquor. Bring slowly to the boil on the top of the stove, uncovered, and let the wine reduce a little. Add ¼ pint/150 ml water. Cover the casserole with a layer of foil and a tight fitting lid. Cook in a preheated oven, 150°C, 300°F for 3½–4 hours.

Skim off some of the fat and remove the bouquet and orange peel before serving.

LOVAGE AND POTATO OMELETTE

This is a substantial omelette, like a Spanish tortilla.

*4 tablespoons olive oil
1 medium onion, chopped
1/4 lb/125 g bacon or cured ham, diced
3 medium potatoes, cooked and diced
4 eggs
a handful of lovage leaves, chopped
salt and pepper*

Heat 2 tablespoons oil in a large frying pan and sauté the onion until golden. Add the bacon and potatoes and cook for 4–5 minutes more. Beat the eggs lightly in a bowl, season to taste, then mix in the vegetables and bacon and the lovage.

Clean the pan well, heat the remaining oil until hot and pour in the egg mixture. Cook over low heat, shaking the pan to prevent sticking. When the eggs are set put a plate over the pan and turn the omelette upside down onto it. Add a little more oil if necessary, then slide the omelette back into the pan to cook for a few minutes longer.

Serve hot or at room temperature, cut in wedges.

TURKISH KOFTE

These kofte can be molded into a sausage shape around a skewer or shaped like hamburgers.

*1 lb/500 g ground lamb
1 small onion, chopped finely
2 teaspoons dried mint
1/2 teaspoon red pepper flakes
salt*

Combine all the ingredients and work to a paste in a food processor. Divide in four and work with wet hands to the shape you wish. Cook under a grill or on a barbecue for 8–10 minutes.

RICE WITH MINT AND CORIANDER

8 oz/250 g basmati rice
a handful of coriander leaves
a handful of mint leaves
2 green chilies
1 onion
1/4 cup/75 ml oil
4 cloves
2 in/5 cm stick cinnamon
1 teaspoon salt

Wash the rice well and let soak in clean water for 30 minutes. Chop the herbs finely; remove the seeds and chop the chilies; chop the onion finely. Heat the oil in a large pan until very hot, add the cloves and cinnamon, then the rice, and stir well to coat all the grains with oil. Add the herbs, chili, onion and salt, pour over 1 pint/600 ml cold water, stir briefly and bring to the boil. Reduce the heat and simmer, covered, for 15 minutes or until most of the water is absorbed and there are holes on the surface. Turn off the heat but leave the tightly covered pan on the hot surface for another 15 minutes. Stir with a fork to avoid breaking the grains, turn out onto a warm dish and serve.

Roasted Garlic

Roasted garlic is best made with new garlic in the summer. It has a mellow flavor that goes well with roast lamb or chicken.

4 heads garlic
2 tablespoons olive oil
salt and pepper

Separate the garlic heads into cloves, but don't peel them. Put them into an earthenware baking dish, pour over the oil, making sure all the cloves are coated. Add salt and pepper to taste and roast in a preheated oven, 180°C, 350°F, for 20–30 minutes, basting from time to time. When done, the soft flesh slips out of the skin quite easily.

Tian of Tomatoes and Eggplant

2 large eggplants
1 onion, chopped
olive oil
2 cloves garlic, chopped finely
a handful of basil leaves
2 eggs
salt and pepper
3 large tomatoes
2 tablespoons bread crumbs
2 tablespoons grated Parmesan

Cube the eggplants and cook in boiling salted water for 5 minutes. Drain and put aside. Cook the onion in 1 tablespoon oil for 10 minutes until soft, then add the garlic. Tear the basil leaves into small pieces. Beat the eggs, season with salt and pepper and stir in the eggplant, onion, garlic and half the basil. Brush a gratin dish with a little oil and pour in the mixture. Sprinkle with oil, slice the tomatoes and arrange them on top. Season with salt and pepper and scatter with the remaining basil. Spread the bread crumbs and Parmesan over everything and add a little more oil. Bake in a preheated oven, 190°C, 375°F, for 35 minutes.

BRAISED ARTICHOKES

4 artichokes
a small bunch of parsley, chopped
1 teaspoon mixed herbs –
marjoram, savory, thyme
1 bay leaf
4 cloves garlic
²/₃ cup/150 ml olive oil
1 cup/250 ml white wine
salt and black pepper

Break off the stalks, remove the tough outer leaves and trim the tops of the artichokes. Put them, stem side down, in a heavy pan in which they just fit. Scatter the herbs and garlic among them. Pour over the oil and wine; and add just enough water to cover. Season, cover the pan and bring to a boil, then simmer for 30–40 minutes. When a leaf pulls out easily the artichokes are ready. Serve with the cooking liquid, reduced by boiling if necessary, as a sauce.

Mint Julep

For each person put *a teaspoon of superfine sugar* and *2 teaspoons of water* into a tall glass and stir to dissolve the sugar. Add *3–4 sprigs of mint*, fill the glass with crushed ice and pour over a large measure of *bourbon whiskey*. Put a couple more sprigs of mint on top and serve with a straw.

Bergamot and Lemon Sorbet

1¼ cups/250 g sugar
1¼ cups/300 ml water
6 sprigs bergamot
1 egg white
²/₃ cup/150 ml lemon juice

Make a syrup by dissolving the sugar in the water and then boiling hard for 3 minutes. Steep the bergamot in the syrup and let it cool. Strain. Whisk the egg white lightly and add to the syrup with the lemon juice. Pour into an ice cream machine and freeze according to the manufacturer's instructions.

Rosemary and Muscat Sorbet

1¼ cups/300 ml water
²/₃ cup/125 g sugar
3–4 sprigs rosemary
1 egg white
1 cup/250 ml muscat

For a rich, sweet muscat flavor use a wine such as Beaumes-de-Venise; for a lighter, dryer muscat taste use a muscat from Alsace. Bring the water and sugar to a boil and boil hard for 3 minutes. Steep the rosemary in the syrup and let it cool, then strain. Whisk the egg white lightly and add to the syrup. Stir in the wine, pour into an ice cream machine and freeze according to the manufacturer's instructions.

INDEX

ACKNOWLEDGMENTS

The publishers
would like to thank the following people:

JACKET
· PHOTOGRAPHY ·
DAVE KING

· TYPESETTING ·
WYVERN
TYPESETTING LTD

· ILLUSTRATORS ·
JANE THOMSON
SHEILAGH NOBLE

DESIGN
· ASSISTANCE ·
SUE CORNER

· REPRODUCTION ·
COLOURSCAN
SINGAPORE